To a friend... 2-14-84

To my #1, "MAINE" Squeeze, William
With all my Love, Colleen

"May your hand be full for always if only with another hand.
May your heart be empty only long enough to give you cause to fill it up again with
  love.
May your soul be lost by you only to be found by God."
—Rod McKuen, singer/songwriter

FRENCH VEGETARIAN COOKING
Simple Recipes by Bernadette

A PERIGEE BOOK

Perigee Books
are published by
The Putnam Publishing Group
200 Madison Avenue
New York, New York 10016

Library of Congress Cataloging in Publication Data

Bernadette.
  French vegetarian cooking.

  I. Vegetarian cookery.   2. Cookery, French.
I. Title.
TX837.B48   1983   641.5′636   83-8322
ISBN 0-399-50841-4

Designed by Terry Jones
First Perigee printing, 1983
Printed in the United States of America
1   2   3   4   5   6   7   8   9

Contents

Les Soupes   9

Les Sauces   39

Les Oeufs   57

Les Omelettes   69

Les Soufflés   83

La Pâte et Les Tartes   99

Les Légumes   125

Les Salades   149

Les Desserts   163

Index   191

I did this book about three years ago, in French, for a friend – a lovely man, a végétarian who was living in New York.

I am not a végétarian myself but, at the time, I found most végétarian food so boring. There are so many delicious végétables to choose from. And I think, too, that you can prepare a lovely meal –good enough to receive friends – with no meat or fish at all. Also, like everybody else, there are times when my purse is empty. So, I worked out all my recipes, and I found that my cooking could be quite inexpensive.

But back to my friend…For his birthday, I gave him this book for a present. I think he was quite pleased, and friends asked him, "Why doesn't Bernadette write the recipes in English?"

So, you know, with me everything takes time – don't forget I am from the South of France. But, finally, just when I did finish the book, it went for a long sleep – for one year and a half – in a cupboard...

However, after remorse, laziness, bad dreams... I took it out, met some very nice people who were ready to help me publish it – and so here we are!

I have written down some of my favourite recipes, and with them I hope you can prepare some good meals – from soupes to desserts, from start to finish. – for you and your friends to enjoy.

Good luck with all the dishes. I do hope you will like them.

Bernadette

Les Soupes

When I have time, I cut the leeks in small pieces and fry them first in 100gr. (3oz) butter. It's more tasty!

Soupe à la paysanne
(serves 6)

Leeks, 2
Onions, 3
Potatoes, 500gr. (1 lb)
Carrots, 1 kg. (2 lbs)
A small cauliflower
Celery, few sticks
Beans, etc...
Fresh herbs.
(If you want — olive oil,
 fresh cream or parmesan
 cheese ...)

Takes all the kinds of végétables you like — and don't forget the herbs. (In winter, fresh parsley and, when in season, thyme, rosemary, etc...)

Cut everything in small pieces and put in a big pan. Cover generously with water. Salt and pepper!

Cover with lid and cook on a low heat for about one and a half hours.

(The végétables shouldn't be too cooked. Following your taste, add some olive oil, fresh cream or fresh parmesan...)

⑪

Not difficult to make. Every English "citoyenne" grows fresh mint...

Potage à la menthe et à la tomate
(serves 6)

Tomatoes, 1kg (2lbs)
Onion, one
Carrot, one
Butter, 60gr. (2oz)
Flour, one big spoon
Sugar, 2 lumps
Fresh mint...

Peel the tomatoes — passed in boiling water first — then brown, in butter, the onion and the carrot, cut in small pieces. Add to it the flour and the tomatoes. Then pour on one litre (about 2 pints) of water. Salt and pepper! Add the sugar. Cook slowly on a low heat for 45 minutes...

When it's cooked, mix, and add a little more water if the soupe is too thick — this will clear it.

When you serve, add in it a little more butter and some fresh mint, cut in small pieces...

If you can, try to get red potatoes, but don't worry, I more often use the white ones. And when it's ready to be served, don't forget the 20 leaves of cress to decorate!

Potage au cresson
(serves 6)

Watercress, 2 bunches
Butter, 40 gr. (1½oz)
Potatoes, 500gr. (1lb)
Single cream, 125 gr.
　(4-5oz carton)
Flour, one small spoon

Mince or finely chop the watercress, taking away before the big stalks, and keep between 10 or 20 full leaves for decoration.

In a pan, melt the butter and add to it the watercress. Warm for a few minutes and add 1½ litres (about 3 pints) of water, and the potatoes, peeled and cut in pieces. Salt and pepper, and leave to simmer for half an hour.

When it's ready, blend everything - and rectify the salt and pepper.

Add to the potage, the fresh cream, mixed with the spoon of flour. Simmer again for a few minutes...

It's ready to be served...

Be careful to wash the leeks very, very well. It's quite difficult to take the dirt away – and it's not very pleasant to eat some grit!

Soupe aux poireaux et pommes de terres
(serves 6)

Leeks, 3
Butter, 100 gr. (3½ oz)
Potatoes, 500gr. (1 lb)
Bread, 12 small slices

Turn to brown the well washed leeks, cut in small pieces, in some butter in a big pan. Add the potatoes, peeled and cut in pieces. Dampen with 2 litres (about 4 pints) of water. Salt and pepper, and cook slowly for 30 minutes...

When it's cooked, mash the potatoes and pour everything in a tureen on the slices of bread, which are grilled or fried before, in butter.

When you serve, add a spoon of butter...

When you serve, add fresh parmesan and some croûtons (fried in butter)...

Potage Rossini
(serves 6)

Onions, 500 gr. (1 lb)
Butter, 60 gr. (2 oz)
Flour, one big spoon
Tomatoes, 3 big ones
Thyme, parsley...

Cut in small pieces the onions and cook them until they form a sort of purée. But don't burn them! Sprinkle with flour, salt and pepper, then add one litre (about 2 pints) of boiled water. Simmer for 30 minutes...

In another pan, reduce the tomatoes with some thyme, parsley... Salt and pepper! Again, when you get a sort of purée, mix all together on a low heat for just a few minutes.

It can then be served...

I use a small tin of tomatoes more for the colour. In winter, the tomatoes are "pâles".

In summer, you can do this soupe with less water and, 15 minutes before you serve, add a handful of ice-cubes...

Potage à la tomate
(serves 6)

Tomatoes, 1 kg (2 lbs)
Tinned tomatoes, one small
    tin
Flour, one big spoon
Butter, 40 gr. (1½ oz)
Single cream, 70 gr.
    (small carton)

Cut up tomatoes, put in a pan, and cover with water. Simmer for 25 minutes, then pour in a strainer rested on a tureen, and squash the tomatoes. Collect the purée and the liquide, and pour everything back in the pan with about one litre (2 pints) of water, and the tinned tomatoes.

Time for salt and pepper! Simmer again...

In a bowl, mix a small glass of water with the flour. Pour in the soupe, mix, and simmer for 5 more minutes. Then add the butter and the fresh cream.

It's ready — but be sure of the salt and pepper!

Try not to use tinned tomatoes in this recipe. In summer, there are red ones — and so tasty!

Potage glacé tomates - concombres.
(serves 6)

One cucumber
Tomatoes, 1 kg (2 lbs)
Flour, one big spoon
Butter, 40 gr. (1½ oz)
Single cream, 70 gr.
   (small carton)
Ice-cubes

    Make a tomato soupe like the page before but very thick, adding less water this time. Add to it the cucumber, cut in very thin pieces — take away the pips beforehand!
    At the last moment, add to the potage a handful of ice-cubes, and serve...

It's a lovely soupe! And it's not a disaster if one of the herbs is missing!

To be served with some slices of buttered bread...

Soupe aux herbes
(serves 6)

Chervil, one bunch
Watercress, one bunch
Sorrel, 200gr. ($\frac{1}{2}$ lb)
One lettuce
Spinach, 250 gr. ($\frac{1}{2}$ lb)
Butter, 60gr. (2oz)
Potatoes, 500gr. (1lb)

Chop very fine or mince the chervil, watercress, sorrel, lettuce and spinach. You get a big pile!

In a pan, melt just over half the butter and add the herbs. Salt and pepper! Everything should become warm and soft. Then add the potatoes, peeled and cut in pieces. Just cover with water and cook for 2 hours on a very low heat.

Mix, warm again, add some more butter and, if missing, more salt and pepper...

It's a marvellous soupe! I always serve it on 24 December, Eve of Christmas, and before my 13 desserts — it's a French tradition.

Soupe aux oignous lyonnaise
(serves 6)

Bread, 12 slices
Butter, 60 gr. (2 oz)
Ouions, 5 big ones
Flour, 2 big spoons
Eggs, 4
Grated cheese — Gruyère
   or Emmenthal,
   150 gr. (5 oz)
Coguac, one glass

Fry the slices of bread in some butter in a frying pan, at least 2 slices per person. Put to one side.

Turn to brown, in butter, the big onions, cut in pieces. Sprinkle with flour, mix, and add some tepid water, (one glass or two). Pour everything in a big pan (except the bread) with 1½ litres (about 3 pints) of salted water. Add pepper, then simmer for 20 minutes...

In a warm tureen, beat the eggs with the grated cheese. Now pour the potage, bit by bit, over the eggs, beating all the time — the soupe will become white! Add the glass of coguac, then the bread on top of it — and serve...

You can use a tureen or some small bowls — as long as they can go in the heat.

Soupe à l'oignon gratinée
(serves 6)

Bread, 12 slices
Butter, 60 gr. (2oz)
Onions, 5 big ones
Flour, 2 large spoons
Eggs, 4
Cognac, a glass
Grated cheese - Gruyère
   or Emmenthal,
      150 gr. (5oz)

Do a good onion soupe - like the page before - but don't add the cheese to the liquide. Pour into a terra-cotta or ovenproof dish.

Float pieces of bread on top and sprinkle with the grated cheese - a lot! Then pass the dish under a hot grill and let the cheese melt...

It's ready to serve ...

My father comes from the region of the "cèps". Their season is September and it's lovely to go to pick them.

I can find them dried here in London, in all the Italien shops in Soho.

You can actually do this soupe with 500gr. (1lb) of any fresh mushrooms - but "cèps" are the large, big, flat ones...

Crème de cèps
(serves 6)

Dried mushrooms, 40gr.(1½oz)
Flour, one big spoon
Single cream, 70gr.
(small carton)

Take the dried mushrooms, washed well, and pour them in a pan with one litre (about 2 pints) of water or stock. Simmer for 30 minutes. (It smell so good!)

Mix the flour with a small glass of water and add to the soupe. Stir all the time until it become thicker! Simmer for a few minutes and add a little more boiled water if the soupe has become too thick!

Adjust with salt and pepper, and add the fresh cream. Simmer for one more second, and serve...

Ten years ago, lots of English and Americans did not know what an artichoke was! What a joke this was at home!

Crème d'artichauts
(serves 6)

Artichokes, 8 hearts
Butter, 200gr. (7oz)
Sauce Béchamel, 1½ litres
    (about 3 pints)—see
    recipe on page 49 —
    and it's 3 times
    the quantity
Milk, ½ litre (a pint)
Fresh single cream, 70gr.
    (small carton)

Boil for a few minutes the big hearts of the artichokes. Then, in a deep frying pan, in butter, cook the hearts lightly. Add to them the Sauce Béchamel and simmer on a very, very low heat for 25 minutes —without boiling!

When it's cooked, squash everything with a fork and add the milk, a little at a time. Heat through, stirring always. When you serve, add the fresh cream — and a little more butter...

In the South of France, in May, you can do this soupe with some wild asparagus. It's a lot of fun to find it!

Crème d'asperges, blanches ou vertes
(serves 6)

Asparagus, 1 kg (2 lbs)
Butter, 200gr. (7oz)
Sauce Béchamel, 1 litre
   (about 2 pints), see
   recipe on page 49 —
   and double quantity
Milk, 2 big glasses
Single cream, 125gr.
   (4-5oz carton)

Take the asparagus, well washed, and cut away the hard pieces. Fry in a pan, in a little butter, lightly, and add the Sauce Béchamel. Cook on a very low heat for 25 minutes, stirring gently. Do not boil! Then blend everything.

Warm again with the milk and, away from the heat, add the fresh cream, and a little more butter.

It's ready to be served...

When you serve, serve apart, in different dishes, some onions, green peppers, tomatoes, and a few croûtons - the lot cut in small pieces!

In summer, it's a lovely fresh soupe!

Gaspacho
(serves 6)

Tomatoes, 1 kg. (2 lbs)
One cucumber
Green peppers, 3
Garlic, one clove
Bread, 2 small rolls
Olive oil, 2 big spoons
Vinegar, a big spoon

Peel the tomatoes (it's easy if you leave them for one minute in some boiling water). In a blender, put the tomatoes with the cucumber, the green peppers (take away the seeds before), the garlic, and the 2 small rolls, dampened in a little water.

Blend everything, then add the oil and vinegar. Salt and pepper! Blend again...

Leave the Gaspacho in the refrigerator for 2 hours before you serve...

Les Sauces

A lovely sauce for asparagus, leeks, steamed fennel...
Lots of people use flour in it, but they are wrong!

Sauce Normande
(serves 4)

Butter, 100 gr. (3½oz)
Double cream, 200gr.(7oz)
   (one large or 2 small
   cartons)

In a small pan, put the butter, cut in pieces, and the cream. Salt! Warm on a very low heat, stirring always with a small whisk...

The butter melts and the cream will become a bit liquide. When the butter has melted, the sauce is not yet warm enough, so leave for just a little longer. Do not boil! Check the salt and pepper!

When it's ready, serve immediately.

It's a marvellous sauce for all the steamed végétables! I love the asparagus with it. It's easy to do, but when I do it, I am a little bit nervous! So don't worry - you are not the only one!

If the egg yolks become too thick, the temperature has risen too high, so add a few drops of cold water. If they froth up but do not become thick, the temperature is too low, so increase the heat a little...

Sauce Hollandaise
(serves 4-6)

Eggs, 2 yolks
Juice of half a lemon
Butter, 200gr. (7oz)

In a small pan or bowl, pour one small spoon of water. Add egg yolks and mix. Salt and pepper! Add a few drops of lemon.

Boil some water in a big pan and put your pan or bowl in it (or use a double saucepan). Be careful, the water of the big pan shouldn't go into the small one! Beat the yolks with a whisk until thicker.

Remove the small pan or bowl from the water and add a big nut of butter. Mix. It will melt. Add another nut - it won't melt any more. Put the pan or bowl back in the bain-marie... and the piece of butter will melt. Add some more butter... and more... until the end of the butter, stirring gently. Serve straight away...

A lovely sauce for végétables! And you can add some
fresh mint or fresh tarragon — whatever is in season...

Sauce Béarnaise
(serves 6)

Vinegar, 1½ big spoons
Shallots, 2
Eggs, 2 yolks
Butter, 200gr. (7oz)

Like the Hollandaise (on page before) but this time you start differently...

All right... In a small pan or bowl, pour the vinegar and add the finely chopped or minced shallots. Warm on a very low heat until the vinegar has almost evaporated. Add one small spoon of water. Add the 2 egg yolks and carry on with the butter as for the Hollandaise... with a whisk...

Good luck!

Use double cream or whipping cream - the latter gives a wonderfully light sauce, succulent for poached eggs and for asparagus...

Sauce Mousseuse
(serves 6)

Eggs, 2 yolks
Juice of half a lemon
Butter, 200 gr. (7oz)
Double cream, 60 gr. (2oz)

A Sauce Mousseuse is a Hollandaise Sauce (see recipe on page 43), to which you add, at the end, the double or whipped cream...

When it's ready, serve immediately!

Very useful sauce for soufflés, tartes and for soupes.
It's also very good with cauliflower, leeks, fennel... and you
can add some grated Gruyère, some grated nutmeg,
or some saffron....

Sauce Béchamel
(serves 4-6)

Butter, 80gr. (3oz)
Flour, 40gr. (1½oz)
Milk, ½ litre (a pint)

Melt half the butter in a small pan, or in a bowl standing in gently simmering water, on a very low heat until it is hardly warm. Then, away from the heat, add the flour, stirring all the time with a wooden spoon.

Back on the heat, pour on the cold milk, bit by bit, and the sauce will become thick. Stir, and it will just begin to bubble. Salt and pepper! Simmer very, very gently, stirring always, and add a little more milk if it become too thick. Do not boil!

Then add the rest of the butter, bit by bit, stirring always. When it's ready - that's when the butter has melted - adjust salt and pepper and serve...

Excellent with some boiled or steamed végétables like leeks, cauliflower, fennel... You cover them with Sauce Mornay and pass them into a warm oven for about 10 minutes...

Sauce Mornay
(serves 6)

Butter, 80 gr. (3oz)
Flour, 40 gr. (1½oz)
Milk, ½ litre (a pint)
Grated cheese - Gruyère
   or Emmenthal,
      125 gr. (4½oz)

Get ready a Sauce Béchamel (like the page before).
Then add the grated cheese. Melt the cheese at the
last minute — but don't boil it!

Use eggs and oil at the same temperature —and don't add the oil too quickly!

Excellent for a "macédoine" of végétables —or with a fresh basket of raw végétables in summer.

You can add, for a change, some garlic purée, or a fresh purée of parsley, or chervil, or chives...

Sauce Mayonnaise
(serves 6)

Egg, one
Dried French mustard,
  one small spoon
Oil - olive oil or "arachide"
  (ground nut oil), one
  small cup
Few drops of vinegar

Separate the egg yolk from the white. In a bowl, put the yolk and add the mustard. Salt and pepper! Beat with a whisk or stir with a wooden spoon. When it's well blended, pour on the oil in a thin stream, stirring quickly all the time. As the sauce thickens progressively, you make the quantity you want (the amount of oil may be varied to your needs).

At the end, stir in the vinegar (or a little lemon juice) to thin it. Adjust salt and pepper, and serve...

I think the olive oil is the most successful oil for salade where a "rustic" flavour is required.

The French use the "arachide" (ground nut oil), too. Some time, you can meet people who hate olive oil. They find the taste too strong…

Salade assaisonnement
(for all types of salade)

- **With oil**: use for all kinds of salade, with vinegar or lemon juice and salt and pepper.
- **With cream**: suits especially lettuce and chicory. Use with vinegar or lemon, salt and pepper and perhaps some herbs.
- **With eggs**: blend with mustard, oil and vinegar.
- **With mustard and cream**: mostly used for beetroots, chicory, celery and green salade. Add salt and pepper.

Never hesitate to add lots of fresh herbs to your dressings — like tarragon, oregano, rosemary, thyme, basil, parsley, dill, chives...

Les Oeufs

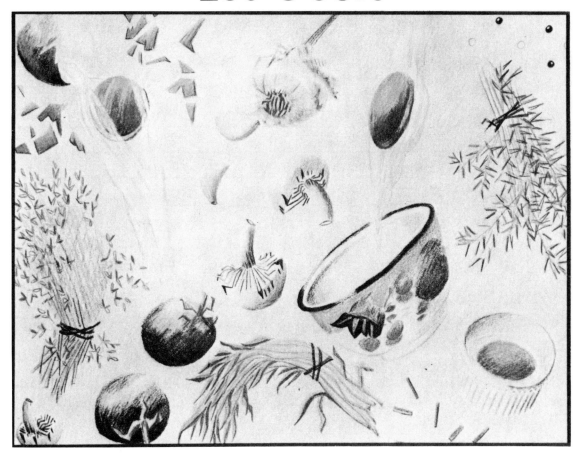

I love them. You can add some slices of black truffles, or different herbs - parsley, basil, fresh thyme, or dill...

Oeufs à la crème en cocottes
(serves 6)

Single cream, 125gr.
  (4-5oz carton)
Eggs, 6 or 12
Fresh tarragon - if you
  want...

Warm six small pots (the same as you use for cream caramel). Pour one finger of very hot fresh cream into pots, then break one or two eggs into each. Salt and pepper! (If you want, put one leaf of fresh tarragon on top of each.)

Cook on a low heat for 2 minutes in a double saucepan or stand pots in a bowl in a pan of simmering water. Then put pots in the oven for 3 à 5 minutes, already heated to 400°F, Mark 6, 200°C. In the oven, the pots have to be covered.

Serve straight away...

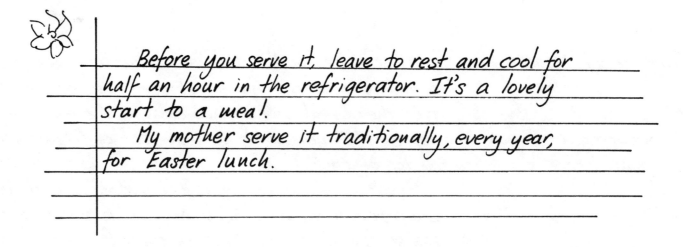

Before you serve it, leave to rest and cool for half an hour in the refrigerator. It's a lovely start to a meal.

My mother serve it traditionally, every year, for Easter lunch.

Oeufs Mimosa
(serves 6)

Eggs, 12
Chopped parsley, a
  big spoon
Sauce Mayonnaise, 3
  big spoons (see
  page 53)
Lettuce leaves for
  decoration

In cold water, in a pan, place the eggs. Leave to boil until you get hard-boiled eggs. Remove from the water and leave to cool. Then peel, and cut each egg in two (on the long way). Remove the yolk and dispose the white 'shells' on top of a bed of lettuce leaves.

In a bowl, put the yolks and, with a fork, mash them to a purée. Then add salt and pepper, a big spoon of chopped parsley and the spoons of Sauce Mayonnaise (see page 53).

Mix everything and, with a small spoon, fill up the holes of the egg whites - generously.

It's ready to be served...

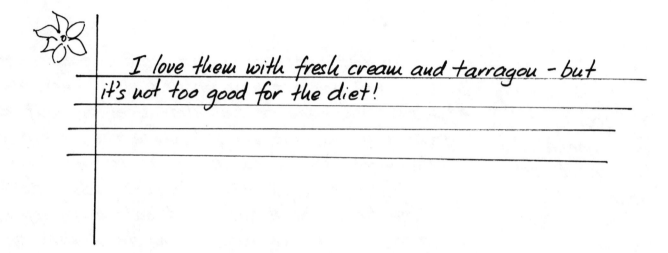

I love them with fresh cream and tarragon - but
it's not too good for the diet!

Oeufs brouillés
(serves 4)

Butter, 100gr. (3½ oz)
Eggs, 8

Warm lightly half the butter in a pan with a thick bottom (you can find one specially for this), or put in a bowl standing in a pan of water over heat. Add eggs and beat — with salt and pepper! Then stir with a wooden spatula on a very low heat. As soon as the eggs are taking on a good consistency — light and fluffy — remove from heat.

Adjust to taste with the rest of the butter, cut in small pieces, and serve...

I always buy my conserved truffles in Spain. They are very good and less expensive.

Oeufs brouillés (suite)

(see recipe on page before..)

Also good with asparagus, mushrooms, croûtons, truffles, herbs, etc...
- Add to the scrambled eggs, 2 big spoons of asparagus, heads only, cooked lightly before in some butter...
- Or 100gr. ($\frac{1}{4}$ lb) mushrooms, well washed, sliced and fried in butter...
- Or fried in butter, without burning, a few small croûtons...
- Or some fresh truffles, well washed and sliced.

If you want, you can add on the top some fresh cream when you serve — and sprinkle with some more parsley...

Oeufs à la pomme de terre
(serves 6)

Potatoes, 6 big ones
Butter, 60 gr. (2oz)
Parsley, chopped, 6 small
    spoons
Eggs, 6

Take and wash the potatoes. Bake them in an oven for one hour at 425°F, Mark 7, 220°c. When they are cooked, cut off the top of each potato. With a spoon, scoop out the inside of the potatoes so you are just left with the shells. Mash the potato 'flesh'. Add the butter, parsley, salt and pepper. Replace the mash in each potato and, on top of each, break an egg. Salt and pepper!

Replace the tops of the potatoes, and bake in the oven, already heated to 400°F, Mark 6, 200°c.

Les Omelettes

To do a good omelette is not so easy, even more so when the flavours are different.

Some like it well cooked, some don't. In fact it should be "moelleuse" (light and soft).

There's no real way to tell you how to do a good omelette. It's just a question of habit. But you require always a very, very good frying pan! And I myself always add 2 big spoons of water when I mix the eggs...

Cook all the time on a low heat — it's a secret of success! By the way, you can also flavour omelettes with mushrooms, Gruyère cheese, onions and sorrel, well washed and cut very fine.

Omelette aux herbes
(serves 4)

Eggs, 8
Butter, 60 gr. (2oz)
Fresh herbs, parsley,
  chives, chervil...

In a bowl, break the eggs. Add half the butter, cut in small pieces, then 2 big spoons of water. Then add some herbs, all chopped finely. Beat the eggs with a whisk. Salt and pepper!

In a frying pan, melt the rest of the butter and when it's very warm, pour on the eggs. With a fork, spread the eggs until the mixture is even. Slide the omelette to the sides of the pan, and when it's ready, lift and fold over. Then serve...

Could be served with lettuce with olive oil and lemon dressing. It will make a nice meal!

Omelette aux croûtons
(serves 4)

Eggs, 8
Butter, 60 gr. (2oz)
Bread, 2 or 3 slices

Always the same principles for omelettes (see page before) but try adding some small cubes of bread, fried in butter, to change the texture. Don't burn them! When they are ready, add to the eggs. Cook as before...

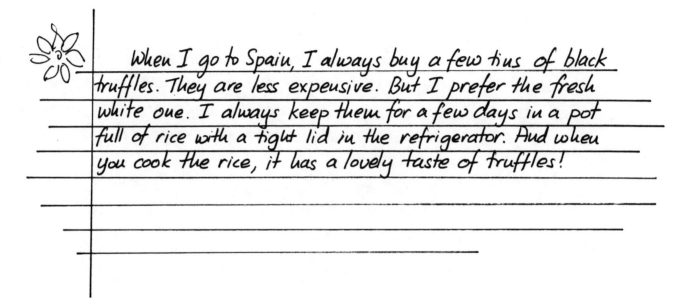

When I go to Spain, I always buy a few tins of black truffles. They are less expensive. But I prefer the fresh white one. I always keep them for a few days in a pot full of rice with a tight lid in the refrigerator. And when you cook the rice, it has a lovely taste of truffles!

Omelette aux truffes
(serves 4)

Eggs, 8
Butter, 60 gr. (2oz)
Truffles, a few

If, by any chance, you have a tin of truffles or, even better, fresh white truffles brought back from Italie by a friend, or fresh black ones from a French friend, slice them on your omelette already cooked.

This recipe came from my Spanish nanny. And, she said, in Spain they serve it some times with a warm tomato sauce on it ...

Omelette à l'espagnole
(serves 4)

Eggs, 8
Olive oil, 3-4 big spoons
Potatoes, 6 small ones
Onions, 2

Again, the same principle as for the 'omelette aux herbes' (see recipe on page 71), but on a low heat, warm 2-3 big spoons of olive oil and fry the potatoes, peeled and chopped, and the onions, cut in pieces, for 20 minutes. They should get soft but not roast.

When they're ready, pour the mixture into the beaten eggs (with the 2 big spoons of water) in a bowl and leave to rest for 5 minutes...

Warm a little more olive oil in a frying pan and pour on to it your egg mixture. Cook on a low heat for 3 à 5 minutes each side.

Serve...

You can also serve the omelette with a purée of
fresh tomatoes alone...

Omelette from the South of France
(serves 4)

Eggs, 8
Tomatoes, 2 big ones
One aubergine or
  egg-plant
Garlic, one clove
Olive oil, 2 big spoons

Blend or finely chop the tomatoes and aubergine (first peel the aubergine!) Add some garlic, peeled and chopped. Cook the végétables to a purée in a frying pan with the olive oil for 5 minutes. Salt and pepper!

Do your omelette as before (see page 71), and when she is more or less cooked, put on it 2 big spoons of the purée and keep a spoonful to put on top of the omelette after you fold and serve it…

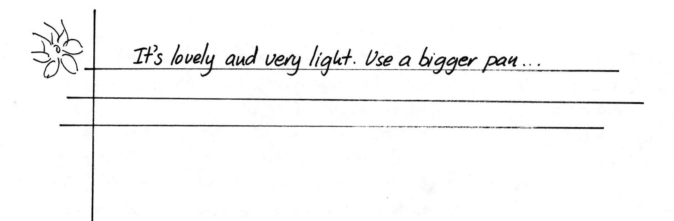

It's lovely and very light. Use a bigger pan...

Omelette de mon ami
(serves 4)

Eggs, 8
Single cream, one big
    spoon
Butter, 20 gr. (1oz)

    In a bowl, mix just the egg yolks with the fresh cream. Salt and pepper! Then beat the egg whites and, when white and fluffy, fold in the yolk mixture.

    Then, on a low heat, cook the omelette as before (see page 71)...

Les Soufflés

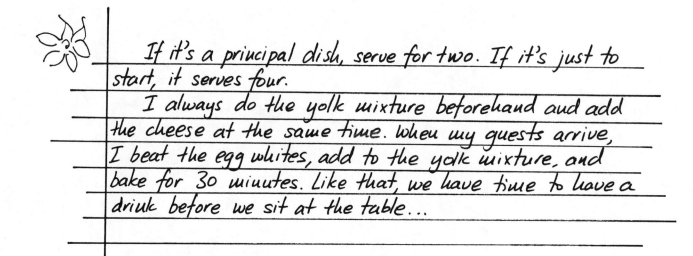

If it's a principal dish, serve for two. If it's just to start, it serves four.

I always do the yolk mixture beforehand and add the cheese at the same time. When my guests arrive, I beat the egg whites, add to the yolk mixture, and bake for 30 minutes. Like that, we have time to have a drink before we sit at the table...

Soufflé au fromage
(serves 2 or 4)

Butter, 60 gr. (2oz)
Flour, 40 gr. (1½oz)
Milk, a glass (½ pint)
Eggs, 4
Grated cheese — Gruyère
    or Emmenthal,
    100 gr. (3½oz)
Nutmeg, if you want

In a pan, melt butter and stir in flour. Right away, add the milk, bit by bit, and stir. Salt and pepper! Bring to boil, stirring always, but at the first bubble, remove from heat. You get a thick 'Béchamel'.

Add a nut of butter, a dash of grated nutmeg — if you want — and the yolks of 4 eggs. Stir with a wooden spoon. Then fold in 3 stiffly beaten whites of eggs and, at the same time, the grated cheese. The mixture can be whipped quite strongly!

Pour in a buttered dish for soufflés, or in individual ones. Bake for 25 à 30 minutes at a temperature (the oven should already be heated) of 375°F, Mark 5, 190°C...

When it's ready, serve immediately!

Recently, I did it for ten persons, like a starter, and I double the ingredients. Wash very, very well the spinach and cook it with no water in a covered pan for 5 minutes.

Soufflé aux épinards
(serves 2 or 4)

Butter, 60gr. (2oz)
Flour, 40gr. (1½oz)
Milk, a glass (½ pint)
Eggs, 4
Spinach, 2 big spoons
   (when cooked)

Do exactly the same recipe as for the "Soufflé au fromage" (page before) but don't use any grated cheese. Instead, add the cooked spinach, blended before or very finely chopped.

Bake as before...

It's a very fine soufflé. I find some of my best mushrooms on the market during all the year. I call them "champignons de Paris" — they are very white and quite small...

Soufflé aux champignons
(serves 2-4)

Butter, 60gr. (2oz)
Flour, 40gr. (1½oz)
Milk, a glass (½ pint)
Eggs, 4
Mushrooms, 250gr. (¼ –½ lb)

Again, exactly the same principles as for the 'Soufflé au fromage' (see page 85), but, instead of the cheese, add the mushrooms, well washed and finely chopped. (Cook them first on a low heat in a little butter.)

Add to the soufflé and bake as before...

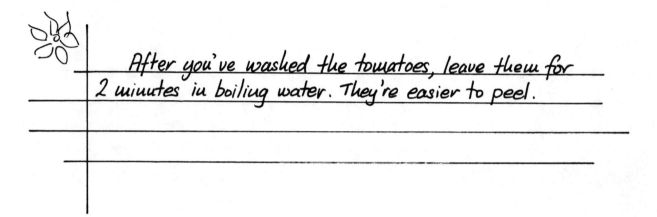

After you've washed the tomatoes, leave them for 2 minutes in boiling water. They're easier to peel.

Soufflé de tomates
(serves 2 or 4)

Butter, 60 gr. (2 oz)
Flour, 40 gr. (1½ oz)
Milk, a glass (½ pint)
Eggs, 4
Tomatoes, 1 kg. (2 lbs)
Olive oil, one small glass
One bay leaf and a
    little thyme...

The same principles as for the cheese soufflé (see page 85), but, instead of the cheese, add tomatoes...

Peel the tomatoes, then cut them in pieces. Warm the olive oil in a frying pan and pour on the tomatoes with the bay leaf and a little thyme. Salt and pepper! Leave to reduce until you get a thick purée.

As before, add to the soufflé and bake for 25-30 minutes at 375°F, Mark 5, 190°C...

I did it for the first time quite recently. My husband was the 'guinea pig' and he loved it!

Soufflé au persil
(serves 4 or 6)

Butter, 60gr. (2oz)
Flour, 40gr. (1½oz)
Milk, a glass (½ pint)
Eggs, 4
Parsley, 2 big handfuls

Again, it is exactly the same principle as for the 'Soufflé au fromage' (see page 85), but, instead of the cheese, add the washed parsley — dry very well and take away the stalks before. Mix and bake as before.

It is simply delicious — and a lovely colour.
Dry well the carrots before you cook them...

Soufflé aux carottes
(serves 2 or 4)

Butter, 60 gr. (2 oz)
Flour, 40 gr. (1½ oz)
Milk, a glass (½ pint)
Eggs, 4
Carrots, 500 gr. (1 lb)
A little more butter —
  about 30 gr. (1 oz) to
cook the carrots

Again, exactly the same principles as for the 'Soufflé au fromage' (see page 85), but, instead of the cheese, wash and peel the carrots and cut them in very, very small slices. In a pan, cook them for half an hour on a low heat in a little butter. When they are cooked, mash them to a purée. Add to the milk mixture, then add the egg yolks and the whites of eggs... and bake as before.

When I did it, I surprised myself. I didn't think it would be so good!

Soufflé au cresson
(serves 2 or 4)

Butter, 60 gr. (2 oz)
Flour, 40 gr. (1½ oz)
Milk, a glass (½ pint)
Eggs, 4
watercress, one bunch

Again, exactly the same principles as for the 'Soufflé au fromage' (see page 85), but, instead of the cheese, wash and mince the cress before adding to the milk mixture. Add the eggs, etc... and bake as before.

La Pâte et Les Tartes

This pastry will keep well for up to 8 days in the refrigerator, in a sealed polythene bag...

Pâte brisée
(medium-sized tarte)

Flour, 160 gr. (7½ oz)
Butter, 80 gr. (3oz)
A little salt

    In a bowl, mix the sifted flour with the butter with the extremity of your fingers –until it become like fine breadcrumbs. Add half a small spoon of salt. Then pour on a little water, not even half a glass. Mix, and when you get a ball of paste, it's ready! It shouldn't stick to your fingers any more and, if it does, add a little more flour...

    It's easy to do, and useful, for more or less every tarte...

If you want to use this pastry to make some small puffs, pipe little round drops of pastry on to a baking sheet, which should be lightly oiled before.

To cook, bake for 15 minutes in the oven, pre-heated to 425°F, Mark 7, 220°C, then 15 minutes more on a reduced temperature — 375°F, Mark 5, 190°C...

Pâte à choux
(makes approximately 20 puffs)

Butter, 80gr. (3oz)
Flour, 125gr. (4½oz)
Eggs, 3

In a pan, pour a big glass of water. Add some salt and the butter. Cook until it's just bubbling - the butter melts! Take away from the heat.

Add the flour and mix very well with a wooden spoon. You have to get a smooth liquide. Cook again on a very low heat for 2 minutes - don't stop stirring!

Away from the heat, add one egg, keep stirring, then another, then another. Incorporate completely.

The pastry is ready. Leave to cool...

My mother, who live in the South of France, taught me this recipe. And with it she makes marvellous pizza! All her students love it.

Proportions are for one medium-sized pizza...

Pâte à pizza
(medium-sized)

Flour, 300gr. (10-11oz)
Yeast, one small packet
   of dried (or, if not,
   just use self-raising
   flour...)
Olive oil, 3 big spoons
Milk, one small glass

Mix the flour with the yeast with your fingers, or just use self-raising flour. Add the olive oil and the milk. Like always, the pastry is ready when it doesn't stick to your fingers any more...

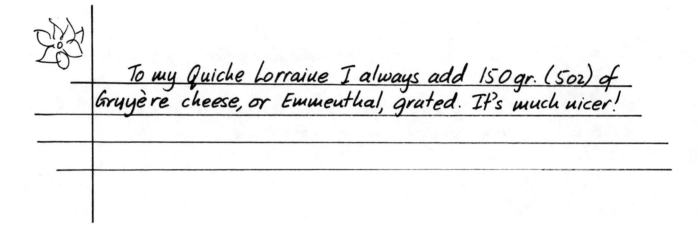

To my Quiche Lorraine I always add 150 gr. (5oz) of Gruyère cheese, or Emmenthal, grated. It's much nicer!

Quiche Lorraine
(serves 4 or 6)

Short pastry, as before
(see page 101)
Single cream, 125gr.
(4-5oz carton)
Eggs, 4
Flour, one small spoon
Cheese 150gr. (5oz)
Nutmeg, optional

Do a short pastry as before (see page 101) and stretch out on a floured surface with a roller (if not a bottle).

Lay the pastry in a buttered pie dish and trim edges.

Mix in a bowl the fresh cream, eggs, some salt and pepper and, if you want, some grated nutmeg - and a small spoon of flour. Add the grated cheese.

Pour the mixture on to the pastry and bake for 30 minutes in an already heated oven at 400°F, Mark 6, 200°C.

Serve hot or cold...

Excellent tarte. Could be a bit heavy for the evenings.
Can be served with a "bouillon" (liquide of a végétable soupe).

I did it the other day and I found that for six people I could add 2 more onions and 2 more eggs...

Tarte aux oignous
(serves 4 or 6)

Short pastry, as before
   (see page 101)
Ouious, 500gr. (1 lb)
Butter, 40gr. (1½oz)
Eggs, 3
Single cream, 250gr. (9oz)
   (2 small cartous)
Flour, one small spoou

Do a short pastry as before (page 101).

Peel and cut in small pieces the ouions. In a frying pan, melt the ouions in the butter. When the juice from the ouions has evaporated and they start to brown, take away from the heat.

Roll out the pastry and lay on a buttered plateau or pie dish. Trim edges. Cover pastry with the ouions and pour over a mixture of eggs, cream and flour.

Bake for 30-35 minutes in an alreddy heated oven at 400°F, Mark 6, 200°C.

Serve warm...

It's a very successful tarte. Perhaps it's one of my favourites!

Tarte aux épinards
(serves 4 or 6)

Short pastry, as before
  (see page 101)
Spinach 1 kg. (2 lbs)
Single cream, 125gr.
  (4-5oz carton)
Eggs, 4
Flour, one small spoon

Do a short pastry as before (page 101), and cook it alone in a buttered pie dish for 15 à 20 minutes in an already heated oven at 410°F, Mark 6-7, 210°C. Put stones or beans on pastry and prick with fork to keep the shape.

Wash the spinach and cook for 5-10 minutes, without water, in a covered pan. Be careful it doesn't burn! If you want, when it's cooked, blend the spinach - it's a question of taste - and mix with the cream. Salt and pepper! Add the beaten egg and flour.

Pour mixture on to the cooked pastry and bake for 15 minutes - or perhaps 20 - in an already heated oven at 400°F, Mark 6, 200°C.

With a bowl of "bouillon" (liquide of a végétable soupe) and an olive oil and lemon salade, it makes a lovely meal!

Tarte au cresson
(serves 4 or 6)

Short pastry, as before
   (see page 101)
Watercress, 3 packets
Eggs, 4 yolks
Goats' cheese – or any
   white cheese,
    300gr. (10-11oz)

Do a short pastry as before (see page 101) and cook it in a buttered pie dish for 15-20 minutes in an oven already heated to 410°F, Mark 6-7, 210°C. Remember to put some stones or dried beans on the pastry and prick with a fork so it keeps its shape.

Wash the watercress and cut out the stalk; chop roughly the rest. Mix the yolks of the eggs, the cheese and the cress. Salt and pepper!

Pour on the cooked pastry and bake for 15 minutes at 400°F, Mark 6, 200°C.

You can serve your tarte with some fresh single cream, apart in a pot, and some fresh chopped parsley...

Tarte aux choux
(serves 4 or 6)

Short pastry, as before
(see page 101)
One white cabbage
Onions, 3
Butter, 40gr. (1½oz)
Thyme, bay leaf...
A little garlic

Do a short pastry as before (see page 101) and cook in a buttered pie dish for 15 - 20 minutes at 410°F, Mark 6-7, 210°C. Do remember to put some stones or dried beans on the pastry so the pie keeps its shape.

In a frying pan, brown the sliced onions in a little butter. Wash and slice the cabbage and mix with the onions. Add the thyme, bay leaf and a tiny bit of garlic. Cook on a small heat for 20 minutes.

Cover the cooked pastry with the mixture and bake for 10-15 minutes in an already warm oven at a temperature of 375°F, Mark 5, 190°C.

Can be served with some fresh tarragon...
My mother serve the mixture some times on
individual buttered toast — one per person.
Note that I use double cream.

Tarte aux champignons
(serves 4 or 6)

Short pastry, as before
   (see page 101)
Mushrooms, 750gr. (1½ lbs)
Butter, 60gr. (2oz)
Double cream, 100gr. (3½oz)
   (from 4-5oz carton)
Flour, one small spoon

Bake the short pastry as before (page 101) in a buttered pie dish for 20 minutes at 410°F, Mark 6-7, 210°C. Remember to put some stones or dried beans on the pastry and prick with a fork so it keeps its shape.

Melt the butter in a frying pan and cook in it the well washed and sliced mushrooms. Salt and pepper! When the juice has more or less evaporated, add the fresh cream, mixed before with the flour. With a wooden spoon, stir the mixture for several minutes, on a gentle heat...

It's ready. Pour mixture on the pastry and serve. (It can be served straight away or put back in the oven again for 10-15 minutes.)

I recommend attention to the washing of the leeks.
You wouldn't like your guests to break a tooth!

Tarte aux poireaux
(serves 4 or 6)

Short pastry, as before
    (see page 101)
Leeks, 1 kg. (2 lbs)
Butter, 60 gr. (2oz)
Sauce Béchamel, 3 big
    spoons (see page 55)
Single cream, a big spoon
Cheese – Gruyère or
    Emmenthal, 200gr. (7oz)

Bake the short pastry as before (page 101) in a buttered pie dish for 20 minutes at 410°F, Mark 6-7, 210°C. Remember to put some stones or dried beans on the pie and prick with a fork so it keeps its shape.

Cook in the butter the very well washed and roughly chopped leeks, taking away the outer leaves before and getting rid of all the grit!

Pour on the cooked pastry a big spoon of Béchamel, then the leeks, then the rest of the Béchamel. Add the fresh cream and a nut of butter.

Sprinkle with the grated cheese and pass under a hot grill for 5 minutes or until the cheese melts.

It's ready to serve ...

Excellent with an apéritif!

Ramequins au fromage
(makes 20)

Butter, 80gr. (2½-3oz)
Flour, 125gr. (4½oz)
Eggs, 3
Grated cheese - perhaps
   Gruyère or Emmenthal,
   for your taste,
   100gr. (3½oz)

Do a choux pastry (see page 103) but when you add the eggs, add the grated cheese as well.

With a small spoon, dispose some small piles of pastry- like big walnuts -on a buttered baking sheet.

Bake for 20 minutes in an already heated oven at 425°F, Mark 7, 220°C.

My mother is the champion for this! We all love it.
She adds to it 1 kg. (2 lbs) of tomatoes, some mozarella
or grated cheese, and oregano...
The tomatoes have to reduce with the onions and,
before you bake, you lay on the mozarella and sprinkle
with oregano...

Pissaladiera
(serves 4-6)

Pizza pastry, as before
   (see page 105)
Onions, 10 small
Olive oil, 5 big spoons
Garlic, thyme, rosemary
Black olives, 100gr. (3½oz)

Lay on a buttered dish the pizza pastry (page 105) and prick with a fork.

In the oil, cook the onions, cut in small pieces, with some salt, pepper, garlic, thyme and rosemary.

Pour mixture on the pastry and lay on it the black olives. Add a little more olive oil and bake for a good half hour in a pre-heated oven at 370°F, Mark 5, 190°C.

Les Légumes

Excellent to start a meal!
I love "girolles" (they are quite yellow with a long stalk), but actually you can use any mushrooms you like. You can use, too, dried mushrooms. You just fry them in butter and add the juice of a lemon – with fresh herbs like parsley or tarragon...

Girolles à la crème
(serves 4)

Mushrooms, 1 kg. (2 lbs)
Butter, 60gr. (2oz)
Sauce Béchamel, 3 big
   spoons (see recipe
   on page 49)
Single cream, 125gr.
   (4-5oz carton)
Juice of one lemon

Wash the mushrooms in a lot of water. Mop them with a tea towel and fry them in the butter in a covered pan, for about 10 minutes. Salt and pepper! Add the Sauce Béchamel (page 49) and some fresh cream (only add the cream if you want!). Leave it to stew slowly — don't boil — and then, at the last moment, sprinkle with the lemon juice.

It's ready to serve...

You can find the small ones in springtime.
   An artichoke is also excellent cooked just in boiling water with a spoon of olive oil and some salt.
   Very good starter. Can also be served with melted butter or a vinaigrette . . .

Artichauts à la provençale
(serves 6)

Artichokes, 6
White wine, one glass
Olive oil, 3 big spoons
Onions, 12 small ones
Tomatoes, 4

Cook for 10 minutes in an uncovered pan the artichokes in plenty of fast-boiling salted water. Out of the water, leave them to cool and, between your two hands, press the water away.

Then in a pan, with a glass of water, the white wine, olive oil, onions and tomatoes, cut in pieces, and salt and pepper, cook them gently on a small heat for about one and a half hours. Then serve with the sauce...

It's delicious, and, if you have some fresh herbs, it's even better – and add some fresh, grated parmesan!

Poireaux à la crème
(serves 6)

Leeks, 1½ kg. (3 lbs)
Sauce Béchamel, a
   few big spoons (see
     page 49)
Paprika, ½ tsp.
Curry powder, ½ tsp.
Cayenne pepper, a pinch
Oregano, one tsp.
Cheddar cheese,
    500gr. (1 lb)

Wash well the leeks and cut in two - on the long way. Wash again. In boiling water, cook the leeks until they get soft. Strain away the water, and lay them in an ovenproof dish.

Do a Béchamel (see page 49) and add in it the paprika, curry powder, the cayenne pepper, oregano — and some salt and pepper. Pour the mixture on top of the leeks and add to them the strong, grated cheese.

Bake for 25 minutes in a warm oven - already heated to 375°F, Mark 5, 190°C.

Serve hot...

Spinach is excellent, too, just cold, with some lemon and olive oil. Or when it's new, fresh and uncooked, in salade with some raw mushrooms...

Épinards à la crème
(serves 6)

Spinach, 2 kg. (4 lbs)
Butter, 80 gr. (2½ - 3oz)
Single cream, 80gr.
  (from one small
  carton)

When the spinach is very, very well washed, cook in a big pan, with no water, for 5 minutes... Drain, and mash with a fork.

In a big saucepan, heat half the butter, and throw in the spinach. Salt and pepper! With a wooden spatula, stir for another 5 minutes, then add the rest of the butter and the cream. Heat a little more and adjust the salt and pepper.

It's ready to be served...

The aubergines can be deep-fried, too. Pass them in some flour to coat them, dampen in beaten eggs and plunge into hot oil for several minutes.

Aubergines à la provençale
(serves 6)

Aubergines (or egg-plants),
   1 kg. (2 lbs)
Flour, enough to coat
   aubergines
Olive oil, 4 big spoons
Tomatoes, 1 kg. (2 lbs)
Garlic, one clove
Fresh parsley

    Peel and cut in slices — large like your small finger — the aubergines (or egg-plants). Sprinkle with a lot of salt and leave for 20 minutes (all the juice will go out). Then dry them with some paper before rolling in the flour.

    In a frying pan, pour the olive oil and fry them.

    In a different frying pan, cooked the chopped-up tomatoes with salt and pepper and a clove of garlic — peeled and chopped.

    When both végétables are cooked, mix together and add the fresh parsley. Serve . . .

When I was a child, I hate them. Now I love them!
If you get some big chicory, cut in two...

Endives à la meunière
(serves 4 - 6)

Chicory, 1 kg. (2 lbs)
Butter, 150 gr. (5 oz)
Juice of one lemon.

Wash and arrange the chicory in a dish (ovenproof) in some warmed butter. Add salt, pepper and the juice of one lemon. Cover with a buttered paper and bake them until they start to turn brown — this takes about one hour in a medium oven — 350°F, Mark 4, 170°C.

Serve hot...

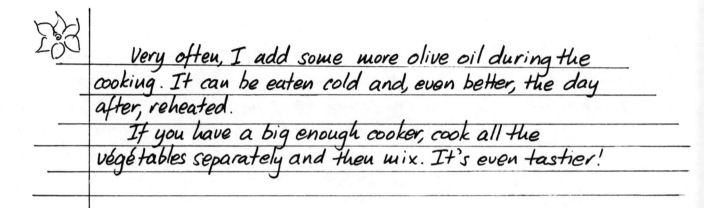

Very often, I add some more olive oil during the cooking. It can be eaten cold and, even better, the day after, reheated.

If you have a big enough cooker, cook all the végétables separately and then mix. It's even tastier!

Ratatouille à la Bernadette
(serves 6)

Onions, 2 big ones
Olive oil, 3 big spoons
Butter, a big spoon
Aubergines, 2
Green peppers, 2
Red pepper, 1
Fresh herbs – thyme,
   rosemary, basil...
Courgettes, 6
Tomatoes, 6

Fry in a big dish – if possible, terra-cotta (tastes better) or simply in a big pan – the onions, cut in pieces, in the olive oil and butter.

When they start to brown, add the aubergines (egg-plants), not peeled but cut in pieces, the peppers, cut in pieces and the core and seeds removed, and salt and pepper! Then add a lot of the fresh herbs – thyme, rosemary, basil...

During the cooking (about half way through), always on a very low heat, add the courgettes and tomatoes and leave to melt... The whole cooking time takes about one and a half hours...

It's a lovely dish, and to make more rich, you can always add some fresh cream and less milk...

Gratin Dauphinois
(serves 6)

Milk, ½ litre (1 pint)
Potatoes, 750gr. (1½ lbs)
Nutmeg, a dash
Garlic, one clove
Egg, 1
Grated cheese – Gruyère
   if possible,
   125gr. (4½oz)
Butter, 60gr. (2oz)

Boil the milk and cool. Peel and wipe the potatoes and cut them in very thin slices. Sprinkle with salt and pepper and a dash of grated nutmeg.

Lay the potatoes in an ovenproof dish, rubbed round with garlic.

Whip the egg and mix with the tepid milk. Sprinkle the potatoes with half the grated cheese, then pour on the milk. The milk should just soak the potatoes.

Sprinkle on the top the rest of the cheese and dot with butter.

Bake for 45-50 minutes in an already hot oven at 400°F, Mark 6, 200°C.

In winter, you can use a tin of petit pois "extra fin"! French or Italien! You add them just before serving... about 5 minutes before.

Jardinière de légumes
(serves 6)

Onions, small ones,
    500gr. (1lb)
A lettuce
Carrots, 500gr. (1lb)
Fresh peas, 2 kg (4lbs)
Butter, 150 gr. (5oz)
Fresh parsley...

In a cocotte or a simple pan, cook in butter some small onions (new ones), the lettuce, carrots, all cut in pieces, then the green peas. Salt and pepper! Add a glass of water.

Cook on a low heat for one to one and a half hours, and cover the pan with a plate full of water (I've always done this).

Sprinkle fresh parsley on top of the végétables when you serve...

For me, they are my favourites!

Les manges-tout

  Excellent végétable. Shouldn't be too cooked. Can
be steamed, or fried in butter or in olive oil.
  If you fry them, don't stop turning them.
"Cuisson" (cooking time) 5 minutes...

The best carrots I ever ate were in Jamaica, prepared by a local woman! A délice!

For the 'carottes à la crème' do the same but, 5 minutes before you serve, add one small pot of single cream and the juice of one lemon...

Carottes à la vichy
(serves 4-6)

Carrots, 1 kg. (2 lbs)
Butter, 80gr. (2½ oz)
Sugar, 2 small spoons
Fresh parsley

Cut in slices (thin) the carrots. Then, in a big pan, melt the butter and add the carrots. Salt and pepper, and add the sugar. Cover them with 2 pints (or one litre) of cold water.

Bring to the boil and cook until most of the water has evaporated — just at the end, they would cook only in the butter.

When you serve, add some fresh, chopped parsley...

Les Salades

It's a very fine salade — and really delicious with all sorts of salty tartes...

Salade d'endives aux noix
(serves 4-6)

Endives, 750gr. (1½ lb)
Nuts, 60gr. (2oz)

Dressing:
Mustard, 2 small spoons
Salt and pepper
Oil, arachide, 3 big spoons
Vinegar, 2 small spoons

Trim and wash the endives, then dry and cut in slices. In a bowl, arrange them, and on top sprinkle the chopped nuts.

Do a mustard dressing. In a bowl, put the mustard, salt and pepper and, as a mayonnaise, little by little, pour on the oil. Mix and then add the vinegar.

It's a very healthy salade. Mix the dressing about 10 minutes before you serve . . .

Salade de lentille
(serves 4-6)

Lentils, 300 gr. (10½oz)
Onions — one for cooking
   and 2 fresh ones for
   the salade
Salt and pepper
Parsley, 3 big spoons

Dressing:
Vinegar, 2 big spoons
Oil, arachide, 3 big spoons
Salt and pepper

Wash very, very well the lentils — in case of stones. Drain, and cook in a pan of boiling water — about 1½ litres (3 pints) — with one onion, salt and pepper, and perhaps some dried herbs if you have some, for about 40 minutes. Drain and leave to cool.

When cold, pour in a bowl and add the raw, sliced onions and fresh, chopped parsley.

Add dressing — and serve...

The mixture of salty and sweet is very pleasant.
This can be done too with fresh pineapple.

Salade de carottes
(serves 6)

Carrots, 750gr. (1½ lbs)
Cheese, Gruyère or
   Emmenthal, 250gr. (½ lb)
Apples, 3
Currants, 60gr. (2oz)

Dressing:
Mustard, 2 small spoons
Oil, arachide, 3 big spoons
Lemon juice, 2 small spoons
Salt and pepper

Peel and grate the carrots. Put them in a bowl, and add the cheese, cut in small cubes. Add the peeled apples, cut too in small cubes. Finally, mix in currants.
   Add at the last moment the dressing – quite heavy with mustard.

This is nice and fresh in summer. To make a change, add with the cream some blue cheese — like Roquefort, for example...

Romaine à la crème
(serves 4-6)

One Cos lettuce
Oregano, 3 small spoons

Dressing:
Single cream, a large
    carton, 250 gr. (8 oz)
Lemon juice, few small
    spoons to taste
Salt and pepper

Buy a nice big Cos lettuce. Wash and dry well, and place in a big bowl, cut in large pieces. Sprinkle with oregano.

Then do the cream dressing, mixing together the fresh cream, lemon and salt and pepper. Turn the salade with the dressing.

157

Don't turn the salade until serving. And don't forget to plant the stones of your avocados!

Salade d'Haricots verts
(serves 6-8)

French beans, 750gr. (1½ lbs)
Mushrooms, 250gr. (½ lb)
Avocados, 3
Parsley, 3 big spoons

Dressing:
Olive oil, 3 big spoons
Lemon juice, 1-2 big spoons
Salt and pepper

In boiling water, put your French beans, topped and tailed, for 5-8 minutes. Drain and leave to cool.

Wash and dry your mushrooms, and cut into fine slices. Peel the avocados, cut in half, take away the stone, and cut into tiny slices.

In a bowl, place all the végétables and then add your dressing. Add the fresh parsley.

Don't turn the salade until the last minute, in front of your guests. It's delicious too with some fresh or dried herbs like thyme, oregano. . . .

Salade provençale
(serves 6 - 8)

Tomatoes, 5
Green peppers, 6
One lettuce
Endives, a couple
Fennel, 2
Rice, 200gr. (7oz)
Eggs, 6
Olives, 100 gr. (3½ oz)

Dressing:
Vinegar, 1 big spoon
Oil, olive or arachide,
   3 big spoons
Salt and pepper

Wash and dry very well the tomatoes, green peppers, lettuce, endives, fennel, then cut into slices — even the leaves of the lettuce if they are too large.

In a big bowl, add the rice — already cooked, drained and cold. Then mix in all the végétables. Nicely, on top of this, arrange the eggs — hard-boiled, cut in halves and cold too — and sprinkle the salade with the olives.

Add at the last minute the vinaigrette.

Les Desserts

It's a very light dessert and I hope now you start to be used to soufflés! When you bake, don't forget the oven shouldn't be too warm and don't open the door during the "cuisson".

The chocolate soufflé is exactly the same recipe, except, in the milk, you melt three slabs of chocolate and just 75gr. ($2\frac{1}{2}$ oz) sugar...

Soufflé à la vanille
(serves 4)

Butter, 40gr. (1½oz)
Flour, 40gr. (1½oz)
Sugar, 100gr. (3½oz)
Milk, a medium glass
Vanilla essence, a few
    drops
Eggs, 5

In a pan, melt the butter and add, with a wooden spatula, the flour. Mix very well over a low heat. Then add the sugar and the milk. Warm... It's like a sugared 'Béchamel.' Add the vanilla and, away from the heat, mix in the egg yolks...

Beat the whites of the eggs very strongly and fold into the 'Béchamel.'

Pour into a soufflé dish, buttered and sugared before. Cook in an already heated oven for 30 minutes at 375°F, Mark 5, 190°C.

Don't use a strong-tasting oil. Eat them warm and right away!

Beignets aux pommes
(serves 6)

Eggs, 2
Flour, 350 gr. (12½ oz)
A little beer
Cooking apples, 500 gr. (1lb)
Ground nut oil or
  "arachide" to fry
  apple rings
Sugar, 60 gr. (2oz)

Make a batter... Mix the eggs with the flour with a wooden spatula. Add the beer, first just a little, mix with flour, then a little more... until you get a liquide like cream.

Peel and core apples and slice in rings. Plunge in the batter and fry the rings, one by one, in some very hot oil.

The fritters are ready when they start to brown. Drain and serve with sprinkled sugar.

You can add some grilled almonds, ground café, or whipped cream on the top...

Mayonnaise de chocolat
(serves 8)

Eggs, 6
Sugar, 6 big spoons
Double cream, 125gr.
  (4-5oz carton)
Chocolat, 3 big slabs
  (milk or plain)

In a bowl, beat the egg yolks with the sugar. Add the cream and mix.

In a pan, melt the chocolat in a half glass of water on a very low heat... Mix, and when the chocolat is melted, take away from the heat and leave to cool a little. Then mix in well the egg mixture and cook again on a very low heat, stirring always. It become thick... don't boil.

Then pour in a big dish and mix the hot chocolat mixture with the whites of the eggs, beaten to a snow.

Leave the 'mousse' to cool in the refrigerator for at least 6 hours!

Don't forget to tell to your friends that the stones are still in the cherries!

I try to use the bitter cherries.

Clafoutis
(serves 6)

Cherries, 500gr. (1lb)
Eggs, 3 yolks and one
    whole egg
Flour, one small spoon
Sugar, 125gr. (4½oz)
Single cream, 250gr.
    (two 4-5oz cartons)
Milk, just a small glass

    In a terra-cotta or ovenproof dish, lay the cherries. Leave in the stones!

    In a bowl, mix strongly the 3 egg yolks and the whole egg, the flour, sugar, cream and glass of milk.

    Pour on the cherries this mixture and bake for half an hour in a preheated oven at 375°F, Mark 5, 190°C.

In the mixture, I always add some water. It's then more light. Allow the mixture to rest for half an hour...

Excellent with sugar, lemon, marmalade, honey, jam, chocolat... And, if you do it for adults, add a small spoon of Cognac to the pan!

Les crêpes
(serves 6)

Flour, 250gr. (9oz)
Eggs, 4
Sugar, a big spoon
Butter, 60gr. (2oz)
Milk, ½ litre (a pint)

In a bowl, pour the flour and, in the middle with your finger or a spoon, make a hole. Break in it the eggs and a pinch of salt. Add the sugar and most of the butter, melted before. Bit by bit, pour on the milk, and stir until the mixture become quite liquide, adding a few drops of water. Leave to rest...

Warm a frying pan and grease with butter (the pan should be chosen well). Pour on some of the batter with a ladle and cook quickly. The crêpes should be thin and transparente! Cook the first side, then turn the crêpes, without breaking, with your fingers, and cook the other side...

Serve straight away...

My children love them and it's not too much work.
You can always do the choux pastry one day before.
They're marvellous, too, with some honey ice-cream!

Profiteroles
(serves 4-6)

Choux pastry, as before
  (see page 103)
Vanilla ice-cream, one
  small pack
Plain chocolat, 2 slabs
Double cream, 70gr. (2½oz)
  (from a small carton)
Eggs, 2 yolks
Flour, one small spoon
Sugar, 40gr. (1½oz)

Do a choux pastry as before (page 103). With a small spoon, dispose small piles of pastry on a buttered baking sheet — the size is up to you. Bake in a pre-heated oven at 425°F, Mark 7, 220°C for 20 minutes or until they turn pale golden. Leave to cool...

At the base of puffs, make an incision with a sharp knife. Fill with vanilla ice-cream. Lay the puffs on a dish and place them in a refrigerator.

In a pan, melt chocolat with a small spoon of water (or 2). Add cream and one glass more of warm water. Mix and bring to boil for one second. In a bowl, mix the egg yolks with the flour and sugar. Add to chocolat and warm on low heat. When thick, pour on profiteroles — and serve...

It's always nice to have some 'crème caramel' in the refrigerator. It keeps for 2-3 days...

Crème caramel
(makes 8 - 10 pots)

Milk, ½ litre (a pint)
Vanilla essence, a few
  drops
Eggs, 3
Sugar, 80 gr. (3 oz)
For the caramel : ——
Sugar, 3 big spoons

In a pan, bring to the boil the milk with the vanilla. Mix in a bowl the eggs and the sugar, then pour on the warm milk. Whip strongly! Set aside.

Do a caramel in an old pan... Melt 3 big spoons of sugar in a big spoon of water. Heat to bubbling. When the caramel turn brown —it's quite a long time — share it out in separate small pots (ovenproof) or in a big dish.

Pour on the pots, through a strainer, the egg mixture. Stand pots in a little water in an old heat-proof dish and bake for 25 - 30 minutes in a pre-heated oven at 375°F, Mark 5, 190°C.

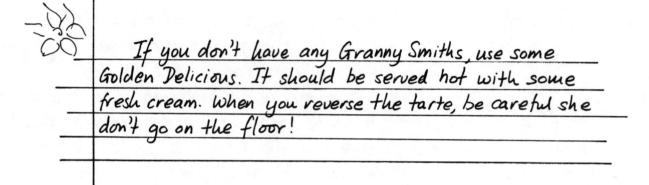

If you don't have any Granny Smiths, use some Golden Delicious. It should be served hot with some fresh cream. When you reverse the tarte, be careful she don't go on the floor!

Tarte Tatin
(serves 6)

Short pastry, as before
  (see page 101)
Apples, Granny Smiths,
  1 Kg. (2lbs)
Sugar, 200gr. (7oz)
Butter, 75gr. (2½ -3oz)

Do a short pastry as before (page 101). In a buttered flan dish, sprinkle some sugar.

Peel the apples and cut in crescents. Arrange them on the sugared dish in a circle. Sprinkle on some more sugar, some pieces of butter and some more pieces of apple in a circle again... some more sugar and butter... The first outside circle of apples is bigger, then a smaller circle, then smaller... Fill in the circle - perhaps four layers will do it.

Lay carefully your short pastry on top of apples. Bake for 45 minutes in a pre-heated oven at 425°F, Mark 7, 220°C. When the pastry is cooked, gently turn the tarte upside down. Add on the top some more sugar and butter. Pass under a hot grill for 5 à 10 minutes.

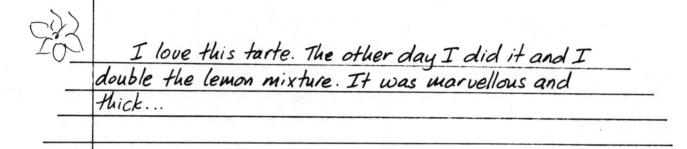

I love this tarte. The other day I did it and I double the lemon mixture. It was marvellous and thick...

Tarte au citron
(serves 4-6)

Short pastry, as before
   (see page 101)
Eggs, 5
Sugar, 150 gr. (5oz)
Lemons, 2
Flour, one small spoon
A little butter

   Do a short pastry as before (page 101). Cook in a buttered pie dish for 20 minutes in a pre-heated oven at 410°F, Mark 7, 210°C. Put some stones or dried beans on the pastry and prick with a fork so the tarte keeps its shape. Cover with a buttered paper.

   Mix in a pan, 5 egg yolks, the flour, half the sugar and the finely grated peel of lemons and the juice. Stir on a very low heat until it becomes thick – like a 'Béchamel'. Then beat the 5 whites of eggs very strongly – like a soft snow – and fold in the rest of the sugar.

   Pour the lemon mixture on the pastry, top with the egg white and bake for 20 minutes in an already heated oven at 375°F, Mark 5, 190°C.

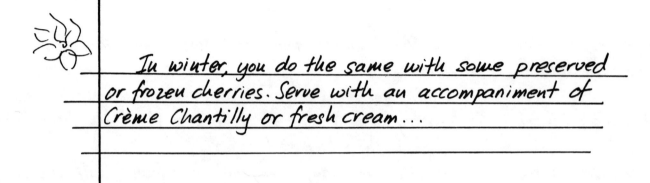

In winter, you do the same with some preserved or frozen cherries. Serve with an accompaniment of Crème Chantilly or fresh cream...

Tarte aux cerises
(serves 4-6)

Short pastry, as before
  (see page 101)
Sugar, 60 gr. (2oz)
Cherries, 500gr. (1lb)
A little butter
Currant jelly, 2 big
      spoons

Do a short pastry as before (see page 101). Lay it on a buttered pie dish, trim, and with a fork prick some holes in it. Sprinkle on it a little sugar. Then, when in season, lay on it the fresh cherries. Don't leave the stones in them! Keep them close together when you arrange them. Dot the tarte with butter and sprinkle with the rest of the sugar.

Bake for 30 minutes in a pre-heated oven at 425°F, Mark 7, 220°C.

Leave to cool and serve with some jam or currant jelly on top.

I don't know one person who doesn't like strawberries tarte. You can use, too, some "fraises de bois"- wild strawberries.

Tarte aux fraises
(serves 4 - 6)

Short pastry, as before
  (see page 101)
Double cream, 125 gr.
  (4-5 oz carton)
Strawberries, 500gr. (1lb)
Currant jelly, 2-3 big
  spoons

Do a short pastry as before (see page 101). Bake in a buttered pie dish for 20 minutes in an already heated oven at 425°F, Mark 7, 220°C. (Don't forget to put the stones or dried beans and buttered paper on the pastry!)

When the pastry is cooked, cool it. Cover bottom with the beaten double cream (or crème Chantilly) and arrange the fresh strawberries. Pour on top some spoons of currant jelly.

I think for a dessert it's too dry, but much nicer for tea. Check on the cooking with a knife, which you insert in the cake. If nothing sticks, it's ready.

Quatre Quart
(serves 4, 6, 8)

Eggs, 3
Self-raising flour,
180 gr. (6½oz)
Sugar, 180gr. (6½oz)
Butter, 180 gr. (6½oz)
Cognac, a small glass

In a bowl, with a spatula, mix the eggs and flour. Then add the sugar and the butter, melted, then the Cognac. The flan mixture is liquide.

Butter one medium flan dish and lay on the bottom one layer of grease proof paper. Pour the cake mixture on it and bake in a warm oven – 400°F, Mark 6, 200°C – for about 25 minutes.

You can see if the cake is ready by introducing a sharp knife inside it — if nothing stick to it, it's ready.

Before you serve it, sprinkle with icing sugar.

A friend did it for me and when I taste it I more or less died — it's fantastic.

Gâteau au chocolat
(serves 6)

Chocolat, 'Bournville' or
'Lindt Bitter', 3 slabs
Eggs, 3
Sugar, 3 big spoons
Non-salty butter,
    250 gr. (9oz)
Flour, 2 small spoons

In a pan, break up and melt the chocolat with one big spoon of water, always stirring — but don't burn it! In a bowl, mix the yolks of eggs with the sugar until smooth. When the chocolat is melted, take away from the heat. Add your non-salty butter, then, through a strainer, add the flour and stir the whole mixture very well. Still away from the heat, add the mixture of eggs and sugar, too.

When everything start to become cold, fold in the stiffly beaten whites of eggs.

Pour everything into an ovenproof dish and cook for 20 minutes, in an already heated oven, at 375°F, Mark 5, 190°C.

Index

Apples
Fritters, 167
Tart, 179

Artichokes
A la provençale, 129
Soup, 33

Asparagus
Soup, white or green, 35

Aubergines
A la provençale, 135
Omelette,with tomatoes, 79
Ratatouille, 139

Beans
Haricots verts salad, 159
Soup, with mixed vegetables, à la paysanne, 11

Cabbage
Tart, 115

Carrots
A la vichy, 147
Mixed vegetables, jardinière, 143
Salad, 155
Soufflé, 93
Soup, à la paysanne, 11

Cauliflower
Soup, à la paysanne, 11

Celery
Soup, à la paysanne, 11

Cheese
With potatoes, 141
Ramekins, 121
Soufflé, 85
Soup, with onions, 27, 29

Cherries
With cream and eggs, 171
Tart, 183

Chocolate
Cake, 189
Mayonnaise, 169
Profiteroles, 175

Courgettes
Ratatouille, 139

Cucumber
Soup, chilled with tomato, 23

Eggs
With cherries and cream, 171
With cream, en cocottes, 59
With mayonnaise, Mimosa, 61
With potatoes, baked, 67
Soup, with onions, lyonnaise, 27
Scrambled eggs, 63, 65
OMELETTES
With cream, de Mon Ami, 81
With croûtons, 73
With herbs, 71
With potatoes, à l'espagnole, 77
With tomatoes and aubergines, 79
With truffles, 75

SOUFFLES
With carrots, 95
With cheese, 85
With mushrooms, 89
With parsley, 93
With spinach, 87
With tomatoes, 91
With vanilla, 165
With watercress, 97
TARTS
Cheese ramekins, 121
Onion, 109
Quiche Lorraine, 107
Spinach, 111
Watercress, 113
DESSERTS
Cake, with cognac, 187
Chocolate cake, 189
Chocolate mayonnaise, 169
Clafoutis, with cherries, 171
Cream caramel, 177
Lemon tart, with meringue, 181
Pancakes, 173
Profiteroles, 175

Leeks
Soup, à la paysanne, 11
With cream, 131
Soup, with potato, 17
Tart, 119

Lemons
Tart, with meringue, 181

Lentils
Salad, 153

Lettuce
Mixed vegetables, jardinière,   143
Soup, aux herbes,   25

Manges-tout
Alone,   145

Mint
Soup, with tomato,   13

Mushrooms
With cream,   127
Soufflé,   89
Soup,   31
Tart,   117

Onions
Mixed vegetables, jardinière,   143
Ratatouille,   139
Soup, à la paysanne,   11
Soup, with eggs and cheese,   27, 29
Soup, Rossini,   19
Tart,   109
Tart, with cabbage,   115

Parsley
Mixed vegetables, jardinière,   143
Soufflé,   93

Pastry
CHOUX
Recipe,   103
Cheese ramekins,   121
Profiteroles,   175
PIZZA PASTRY
Recipe,   105
Pissaladiera,   123

SHORT
Recipe,   101
Apple tart,   179
Cabbage tart,   115
Cherry tart,   183
Leek tart,   119
Lemon meringue tart,   181
Mushroom tart,   117
Onion tart,   109
Quiche Lorraine,   107
Spinach tart,   111
Strawberry tart,   185
Watercress tart,   113

Peas
Mixed vegetables, jardinière,   143

Peppers
Ratatouille,   139

Potatoes
With cheese, Dauphinois,   141
With eggs,   67
Omelette,   77
Soup, aux herbes,   25
Soup, à la paysanne,   11
Soup, with leeks,   17

Salads
With carrots,   155
With endives,   151
With Haricots verts,   159
With lentils,   153
With lettuce,   157
Mixed, with rice, eggs and olives,   161

Sauces
Bechamel,   49
Bearnaise,   45
Hollandaise,   43
Mayonnaise,   53
Mornay,   51
Mousseuse,   47
Normande,   41
Salad seasonings,   55

Sorrel
Soup, aux herbes,   25

Spinach
With cream,   133
Soufflé,   87
Soup, aux herbes,   25
Tart,   111

Strawberries
Tart,   185

Tomatoes
Gaspacho,   37
Omelette, with aubergines,   79
Ratatouille,   139
Soufflé,   91
Soup, chilled with cucumber,   23
Soup, with cream,   21
Soup, with mint,   13
Soup, Rossini,   19

Watercress
Soup,   15
Soup, aux herbes,   25
Soufflé,   97
Tart,   113